W9-BWI-288

ONIONS AND ROSES

ONIONS

AND

ROSES

By

VASSAR MILLER

WESLEYAN UNIVERSITY PRESS

MIDDLETOWN, CONNECTICUT

Some of these poems have previously appeared elsewhere. For permission to reprint and for the assignment of copyrights, grateful acknowledgment is made to the editors and publishers of *Burning Deck, Harvest, Hiram Poetry Review, Hollins Critic, Penny Poems, Southern Poetry,* and *Transatlantic Review;* also to Louisiana State University Press, publisher of *Southern Writing in the Sixties* edited by John William Corrington and Miller Williams.

Library of Congress Catalog Card Number: 68–27544

Manufactured in the United States of America

FIRST EDITION

to Stephen

Contents

I

On Opening One Eye   11
The Protestant Cemetery in Florence   12
The Descent   13
The Wisdom of Insecurity   14
Interim   15
The Calling of the Names   16
Beat Poem by an Academic Poet   17
On Not Making a Retreat   18
Speculation   19
Embarrassed   20
Cologne Cathedral   21
For Honesty   22
Oblation   23
To Jesus on Easter   24
Message from a Burning Bush   25
Lullaby After Christmas   26
Pontius Pilate Discusses the Proceedings
     of the Last Judgment   27
Thus Saith the Lord to the New Theologians   28
De Profundis   29

II

Sick Dog   31
Exercise in Remembering   32
Adoration   33
The Oddballs   34
Lady of Leisure   35
Bitterness   36
For a Bereaved Father   37
What the Cicada Says   38
Sloth   39
For a Dog   40

Change   41

May Mourning January   42

Remembering Aunt Helen   43

Delayed Gratitude   44

In a Land of Indistinct Seasons   45

Dubious Advantage   46

Dirge in Jazz Time   47

With No Strings Attached   48

III

If Beauty Be in the Beholder's Eye: An Elegy   49

Travel Light   50

Meditation After a Death   51

In Faith   52

Elegy   53

Addict   54

Entreaty   55

This Is the Way It Goes   56

Temporary Relief   57

Ecclesiastes the Second   58

Renewal   59

And   60

Modesty   61

The Farm   62

Sophistication   63

On Approaching My Birthday   64

Slump   65

Philosophy of Time   66

Unteachable   67

Fait Accompli   68

Toward the End   69

Invocation   70

ONIONS AND ROSES

I

On Opening One Eye

Dear Lord,
        forgive me if I do not wake just yet
although the air unrolls its silk
to ripple in the sunlight wavering through the milk-
gray clouds; although in the lithe grass, all stubby legs,
puppies and kittens tumble, living Easter eggs;
although the morning flows
over my eyelids shut and graceless,
dear Lord, forgive me, if I seek repose
from night, the nurse who, dark and faceless,
lays me on her dry breasts without a song.
I will wake before too long,
and over my lean and Lenten ribs
put on, more delicate than spiders' webs,
dear Lord, Your satin day,
and go my way.

The Protestant Cemetery in Florence

Exiled with you a moment on this island
Whose lushness folds the stark bones of the dead,
I envy you your breathless flight to Florence,
Till I recall that nothing's quite so simple,
That tables turned will wrench the stoutest heart.
For I remember how you in a letter
Wrote, "Father could have kept me had he loved me
More openly,"—dark secrets future doctors
Would probe for offered on your outspread palm.
And you took morphine till the day you died,
Though less than formerly, Italian sunshine
More curative in poems than in life.
You sought out conversation with the spirits,
An anodyne to heady draughts of flesh
Under whose influence you conceived a child,
A fact to scare a small Victorian girl
Of forty-some-odd years more than ghosts could.
"And I, who looked for only God, found you,"
You sonneteered to Robert, paying God
Rather a backhand compliment that even
A jealous Jehovah would not mind much,
Since Robert himself proved scarcely sufficient.
You looked behind you always, back toward death
Wherein alone you could have borne to hear
Your brother's name, love never having borne
The heavy past away. So I pronounce
Your epitaph carved from the facts which arch
Your grave, "Nothing is final. Only this."

The Descent

I have left the world of the photograph
taken a year and a heartache ago,
where contentment incarnated in sunlight
that was harsh in its heat but innocent
with hope that the next day would not be hopeless,
where my dog laughed in the Eden of her dumbness.
I have left all that behind as I go
into the bloody and furious darkness,
rotten with the skeletons of delight
tortured into despair, loud with their ghosts,
tomorrows decayed into yesterdays.
As I go down where God Himself is only
the solution to a thorny equation,
the distant disturber of twitching shadows,
I say to you what I tell my own heart,
"Goodbye, goodbye, expect me if you see me."

The Wisdom of Insecurity

There's no abiding city, no, not one.
The towers of stone and steel are fairy stories.
God will not play our games nor join our fun,
Does not give tit for tat, parade His glories.
And chance is chance, not providence dressed neat,
Credentials hidden in its wooden leg.
When the earth opens underneath our feet,
It is a waste of brain and breath to beg.
No angel intervenes but shouts that matter
Has been forever mostly full of holes.
So Simon Peter always walked on water,
Not merely when the lake waves licked his soles.
And when at last he saw he would not drown,
The shining knowledge turned him upside-down.

Interim

I play in my delight
the waters of my innocence
serene and white

as flesh and blood condense
to wind and sunlight; for awhile,
dear Lord, dispense

with rigor for a smile.
The only enemy that harrows
employs as guile

the whisperings of sparrows
for which as for her fallen daughters
the silence sorrows

and for my dreams, frail floaters
on some stray breath from Eldorado
fading away when Thy bright shadow
darkens my waters.

The Calling of the Names

I move from room to room.
No one is here to haunt my empty house
except the small dog dancing at my feet,
brown shadow of a loneliness,

which has no other name,
so like a child that cannot tell you his,
or else will not (who knows the difference?)
and sulks and will not say his prayers;

or like an old, old man
who has long since forgotten what he was
assuming that he ever knew, for he
was the demoniac whose name was Legion.

So, I have ceased to call.
No name has magic, summons not one ghost,
which never was, as quiet haunts my house,
Pan's pipe to which the small dog dances.

Beat Poem by an Academic Poet

Birds, birds, birds
burst from the trees, from a feeble beginning
like a bundle of sticks lit under a pot
crackling and sputtering
to the great gorgeous bonfire of sunrise
exploding far overhead
like a high hallelujah.

Birds! their wings
tickling my stomach instead of butterflies
wavering wanly; in bones, belly, blood, flapping,
Get up, get up,
till I do, chanting, by God and by glory
if you can't lick 'em, join 'em,
though body weeps dry tears.

On Not Making a Retreat

The nuns walk by in twos,
Lightly, in heavy shoes.
The nuns send praises thronging,
Their strong wills leashed and longing.

Their voices rise and fall
Washing against the wall
Of the world day after day
Till it has worn away.

The nuns hide like a knife
Under black robes red life,
But never by night betrayed,
Feeling now lust's bright blade

Slipped from its sturdy sheath
Of charity and faith,
Dislodged by the pulse afresh,
Burrows through bone and flesh—

I passing by, austere
As they whose home is here,
My lonely feet refuse,
Lightly, their heavy shoes.

Speculation

These streets as dull as, more familiar than
the lines in my own palm I never read
might have been strange, mysterious as
the streets of Istanbul. My neighbor who
picks up his evening paper might have proved
the object of my pensive interest
(I passed a man in Munich working in
his yard and mused how I had seen him
the first and last time—an incarnate transient).
But for the grace of genes and chromosomes
I might have walked about with different luggage
of language, skin, and heritage. I might
have come to my door and, on meeting me,
have pitied the poor creature standing there,
"How awful to be you!" and gone my way.
I still remember saying to my aunt
one time, "Why am I me?" and she supposing
that I had turned a much too youthful Job
burst into tears. Or maybe she had glimpsed
life's mundane craziness we
hid from each other in a game of rummy.

Embarrassed

Lord! Some assurance, please,
that I who kneel before this altar,
molding these few moments the shape of supplication,
am not gaping upon my own face in a mirror
all, all too clearly,
yet catwise pawing behind the glass for
the cat not there.

Yes! Grant some assurance
that I will not be blown out like
a match that has been struck against Your careless heel
to light Your mysterious purposes a little while;
that I am not
merely one more inexplicable pimple
upon the cosmos.

Why am I here if I
must pose such questions to the darkness
whence no heavenly fire consumes my offering.
No propriety of an Amen ends my prayer.
I stumble from
this wrong room while my apologies
freeze my tongue tight.

Cologne Cathedral

I came upon it stretched against the starlight,
a black lace
of stone. What need to enter and kneel down?
It said my prayers for me,

lifted in a sculptured moment of imploring
God in granite,
rock knees rooted in depths where all men
ferment their dreams in secret.

Teach marble prayers to us who know no longer
what to pray,
like this dumb worship's lovely gesture carven
from midnight's sweated dews.

For Honesty

Better the dark blasphemies of the blood
Than the oblations made of tissue paper.
You have preferred the sullen heart too holy
For hallelujahs piped upon tin whistles.

Pardon me, Lord, all my too ready praises
While I dispraised You on some easy joy,
Pompous red carpet on some glib thanksgiving.
Better Your honor bleeds upon my cobbles,

Your cry of dereliction twisted in my guts
Into reproof and rage, damning me blessed
And crossed for good against a lie, stone-sealed,
Lest I should rise, a puppet from a shoe box.

Oblation

I kneel,
my heart in my hands—
a cold fish,
a stale loaf.

What are
these among so many?
Lord, Your business
is to know.

I rise,
my body a shell
heavy with
emptiness,

You whom
worlds cannot contain
not disturbing
one pulse beat.

My bones
being boughs aflame
with Thy glory,
Lord, suffices.

To Jesus on Easter

You see the universe, as I see daylight,
opening to your heart
like fingers of a little child uncurling.

It lies to you no more than wood to blade,
nor will you tell me lies.
Only fools or cowards lie. And you are neither.

Not that I comprehend You, who are simpler
than all our words about you,
and deeper. They drop around you like dead leaves.

Yet I can trust you. You resembling me—
two eyes, two hands, two feet,
five senses and no more—will cup my being,

spilling toward nothingness, within your palm.
And when the last bridge breaks,
I shall walk on the bright span of your breath.

Message from a Burning Bush

See me, for I am as plain
as the nose on your face.
Look for me and discover
my promises abandoned houses.
Call me, and I will blow like a chill
through the holes in your heart.
Do not know I am here, and I lurk
hopelessly entangled among your echoes.
Snub me within the whirlwind of joy,
for why should you need me
when laughter's my double and life's
my identical twin?
Scorn me who scorch in the fires of your pain
where I burn to a crisp,
to a mocking cinder.
Yet be dumb at noontime and I
shall marry you like your own shadow
till no one can tell us apart,
not even ourselves.
None of your friends but increases
with your backwash of love.
You cannot even dedicate me a song, not a whisper,
unless every light breeze
bears it away.

Lullaby After Christmas

Little Child, sleep softly.
Mary's lullaby,
Worship of the shepherds,
Anthems from on high
May postpone the message:
You are born to die.

Little Child, sleep softly
To the tinkling coffer
Of the Three Kings bearing
Gifts they humbly offer
Lest the myrrh remind You
You are born to suffer.

Little Child, sleep softly.
Ass and sheep adore You,
Hoping that their breath may
Warm the way before you.
Sharper than the horns of
Oxen, nails will gore you.

Little Child, sleep softly.
Blood of babies slain
Near Your crib foreshadows
Yours in its deep stain.
Even God has right to
Peace before His pain.

Pontius Pilate Discusses the Proceedings
of the Last Judgment

Unfortunate. Yet how was I to know,
appointed to preserve the Pax Romana,
that *he* was not another of these fools
whose crosses bristled on the hills like toothpicks.
And how were you to guess that the young girl
you burned one day in France for hearing Voices
was destined to be hailed as saint and genius,
not merely silly in the head from sex?
Most of her kind would be. And it's the duty
of men like us to save the world from madness.
Never mind who saves the world from sin.
For madness does the harm that we can see,
strangles the baby, sets the house on fire,
and rapes the women in the name of powers
we can't, nine times out of ten. And if
we're wrong the tenth time, why should we be blamed?
That judge, now, over there, he'll sit in honor
simply because he happened to follow the way
his nose led him to declare the fellow
who knelt barefooted at the Communion Rail
in a suburban parish a poor crazy
son-of-a-bitch. He bet on a sure thing
and won. Our gambles looked the same. We lost.
He really and truly was the Son of God?
I'm not surprised. The gods will play some joke—
and then get angry every time it works!

Thus Saith the Lord to the New Theologians

Whatever happens, God is no contender,
Whatever happens, God is on the spot.
In all the murkiness, in all the splendor
God is involved, and so says God, "So what?"

Mine were the hammers that built the Tower of Babel,
Mine the tongues muddled that made the going tough
Until it tumbled down. It's in the Bible!
If you don't see it, you don't look close enough.

For after all, did I not make the Devil?
If you agree, you're apt to lose your soul
Only because one lunge past Good and Evil
To where I am will land you in a hole.

He who bears witness of my might speaks truly,
He who denies me, lying, does not lie.
I count no one obedient, none unruly.
I do not have to. I am God Most Sly.

Bicker your brains out, I am none the poorer.
Defend, defy, call me true, untrue.
Hold dialogue, be sure that you're no surer.
Whether you win or lose, I always do.

De Profundis

O Lord, defend me when I go
Through the dark in daylight.
Be with me when I smile peaceably
though tigers tear at my guts.

Stay with me who talk to my friends
as an earless monster
winks at me; comfort me, starved and black-tongued,
though I eat at dainty tables.

Stand by when snowfalls of words melt in
deserts of my deafness.
Sustain me, though morning after morning,
I take life from You like death.

Accept me, though I give myself
like a cast-off garment
to a tramp, or like an idiot's
bouquet of onions and roses.

II

Sick Dog

"Man is the only animal that knows he must die."
Whoever spoke thus never saw a sick dog
baffled, bewildered,
sniffing death in the wind.

If I look like that, liquor is only
lapping my brain, yet one day I will lie staring
stupefied, stunned,
dumb before doom.

Sometimes I wonder whether the sky is God's wide gaze
embracing me as mine embraces my dog
bowed, burdened under
unendurable strangeness.

Exercise in Remembering

The day, holding its breath
under the sweltering sun,
has breathed never a sigh.

Summertime of decay,
proof of spring's false promises,
the green already fades.

How fitting this season
you lay, your life rotting in you
with the sounds in your throat

incomprehensible
to us as are the cicadas'
or ours to one another

so that I felt relief
to see your existence wrapped up
in death's lying precision,

pomp prayed and sung,
then given discreetly to
the lithe ruin of worms.

Adoration

The afternoon is beautiful and silent.
The white garage lifts like the cloudy pillar
Into the sunlight. The tree rears taller,
Its foliage ruffled like a green swan's plumage,
A sudden bird goes skimming through the sky
As noiseless as a fish swims in the sea,
When everything is far and near at once,
Remote as memory and luminous as now,
Till mind is cut adrift and like a web
Shimmering rides the heat waves up and down.
Nothing is half so tenuous as flesh,
Which, on the lightest pretext, steals away
To sleep in the cocoon of summer heat and haze,
When a jay's scream might tumble the brick wall
Next door to slide into the forests of the grass,
The afternoon so beautiful and silent.

The Oddballs

They spill like water in between the fingers,
Since we forget them once they're lost from view.
A tone of voice stays, an image lingers,
A shadow hovers. Soon these vanish too.

No one's at fault. We only stretch so far.
We're not so many minor hounds of heaven.
Leave them to God who tends to sun and star.
Our hands are full from seven to eleven.

But still they haunt us, set our memories aching
From time to time, like children pale and tragic,
Waste products of the world, blown shavings taking
Life from some baleful, accidental magic.

Lady of Leisure

Life never gave her any tasks
Lest labor should unnerve her.
People, she thought, were but the masks
Put on by life to serve her.

Existence was a blessed blur,
Time made a happy hum.
Waiting for life to wait on her,
She waited what might come,

And waited. Sure enough, one day
Life, servant born and bred,
Tripped in with death upon a tray
Like John the Baptist's head.

Bitterness

The old man coughs every morning
as if he would spit up his life
whose sputum clings to his lungs.

The dog whines, rattling her chain,
not comprehending her crime
when her occupation is to love.

The baby cries in his crib,
but can tell nobody the reason,
since grief requires no credentials.

The woman stripped from her dreams
shudders at loneliness each day
laid out for her like a dress.

The wind chimes waken to music
as if such sorrows nowhere existed,
but wind has always been callous.

For a Bereaved Father

No one can touch you
locked in the burning house of your sorrow,

where, far away,
no love or pity can lift a finger.

Jauntiness slung
over your shoulder, you have gone in,

and all the tears
of the angels cannot quench the blaze.

Wry little man,
sparse and dry as the hull of a nut,

Should He see to it,
your loss repaired would beggar the Lord.

What the Cicada Says

The cicada unwinding
his thin green string of song
tosses me a ribbon
if only I could catch it,

follow it as it leads
to a magic world where
pleasure and melancholy
merge, one river of feeling,

wherein to plunge myself,
dive down underneath waves of
flowers and foliage, splash in
fountains of yellow windfalls,

wherein, water-shrunk
to an ear, I might find
that the cicada says nothing
but my name and my home.

Sloth

Sloth is the summer sin
when the soul is smug
as a sunning cat
and hides herself beneath
the green docility
of shade, where growing fat,
smirking her innocence,
she makes my shadow seem her habitat.

For a Dog

You lie there, not sleeping,
only looking at me,
who dare not impute to you thought
and dare not deny it.

Your mystery
deeper than any thinking,
you being more brief than a breath
in man's cut-off sentence,

how should my mind plumb it?
The presumption, the effort
would be tearing a dewy web
with hands always too heavy.

If I said that you
were simply adoring
my face, you would not mind it, even
though I were mistaken,

though you would not know
how to excuse my pride
wishing I could worship, like you,
my whole heart in my eyes.

Change

I can remember
the sun as a great golden eagle
spreading its wings to my will.

Now it moves slowly,
a buzzard drifting across the sky
over the carrion earth,

or swoops, a hawk,
to seize the heart of a newborn puppy
dropped from his pain-crazy mother.

Now I give thanks
if its claws, absent-minded, release me
into some weed patch of sleep.

May Mourning January

He dwindles to the thin cry of a bone
she cannot hear for clamors of her grief.
He lies somewhere beneath her fogs of mourning,

if he lies there, instead of having been
mirrored in long-dead faces, now become
the shrunken shadow of their recognitions.

She clapped her hands and he, a poor old ghost,
jerked upright one more time for a child's whim.
His flesh, like a dry stick, flamed up, then fell,

and she cries for a plaything past repair.
Him none laments because no one remembers
the man the seasons buried years ago.

Remembering Aunt Helen

Dimly remembering how your life made
pious abstractions dance in flesh and blood
and stern negation gentle to a child—
my heart breaks into rainbows of hosannas
hovering around the memory of your head.
Remembering how somebody said, "Why, Helen
could ask me anything. I wouldn't mind."
I see that even timid hearts take courage
Under the uncondemning gaze of kindness.
Remembering how you told a little boy
who asked to buy your cat, "Honey, we don't
sell what we love," I think how most old maids'
affection for their pets is loneliness,
while yours was charity. The daily dust
your footstep stirred became a cloud of glory.
The dust I kick up irritates the nose.
What shall I do then? Shun strong drink as you did?
Read Scripture every night? Keep Sunday strictly?
Or practice with a different set of gimmicks?
Eat fish on Friday? Go to Mass each morning?
Or else fall into trances? Speak in tongues?
Remembering you, I think not. Although poets
grow beards, get drunk, and go to bed unmarried,
their imitators pull the selfsame antics
and never make it, because poems never
spring out of opium. So sanctity
changes its wardrobe at the wearer's will
not to be copied by poor little oddballs
playing their games of holy-holy-holy.
Remembering you, I weep because I find
the skirts discarded but the dancer vanished.

Delayed Gratitude

Become the friends of small things, I take
crickets and gnats for topic,
even the ant arched by my dog's armpit.
for whom I will write an epic

and thereby give him a voice which none
ever did for the ant,
even the Lord who made vocal chords,
creation somewhat aslant.

But he shall surely speak through my verses,
(you can like it or lump it)
the ant no child hears with ears still magic.
My poem shall prove his trumpet.

For he earns it, he and every other
animated caprice,
to me even their limited warfare
being a gesture of peace.

In a Land of Indistinct Seasons

Someone has opened a crystal pane
somewhere in the air
to let the summer out
and the autumn in.
But the leaves putting forth
no single scarlet tongue
are darkly green and silent
about their dying.

Dubious Advantage

Sniffing inside the box
from which her whelps have gone, poor dog,
she whines a little.

I set the box outside
so that her memories will melt
in sun and wind.

If my heart were only
a box! But I belong to man,
lone animal

that prophesies its death,
or, suckling images and shadows,
defines its dying.

Dirge in Jazz Time

FOR SOPHIE TUCKER

Her voice forever match to dry wood
Since, a girl, she sang for a crust,
Her innocence even then understood
As a subtler word for lust
As in age her wisdom would mean delight—
Red-hot Mama who is cold tonight.

Her voice in the veins of every man
Like radiant fire would glisten
Till his body, tuned ear, did nothing else than
Keep cocked to her tones and listen.
But the lilt in his bones has taken flight,
Since Red-hot Mama is cold tonight.

"One of these days you'll miss me." Oh yes,
Though they couldn't credit it then
That she who had flashed in a sequined dress
And danced in the nerves of men
Should have given them this terrible slight,
Not Red-hot Mama grown cold tonight!

Turn the spotlight off of the night-club floor.
Let the jazzmen muffle their drums
And their saxophones she will hear no more
Where winter forever numbs,
Where no one can warm her whose heart burned bright,
Where Red-hot Mama is cold tonight.

47

With No Strings Attached

I remember my dogs who have died,
their hairy shapes lumbering
into the fragility of death,

Their wagging dumbness turned eloquent,
saying, "Think how we tutored you
in tenderness for its own sake,

no reward for kindness promised,
not even by Francis, who
bid birds praise God without saying why."

III

If Beauty Be in the Beholder's Eye: An Elegy

The fishing boat drifting
across the lake
like a ghost,

the little does staring
balanced like six
startled miracles,

the docile hills springing
up, up toward wildness
like Monday turned magic,

this loveliness your
locked lids diminish
by minutest arcs.

Travel Light

FOR ANNE

It would be best to travel light
Between the darkness and the light,
From light of sun to blaze of star
Wherever many mansions are
Or are not, being past our sight
Between the darkness and the light.

You kept it simple, friend most dear,
As you were told that time of year
The leaves fall like the evening rays
Shed from the golden bough of days
Shining upon us cool and clear,
Keeping it simple, friend most dear.

No, not that we have had one word
Of what no ear has ever heard—
The chime of seven seals all broken
In austere Heaven to betoken
Our dusked hall traversed by a bird
Save that your memory brings the Word.

Meditation After a Death

The whole night sky seems to move,
but it is only the little clouds
ambling along the sky like woolly dogs.

Where shall I look for you now
when I think of the stars no longer
as silver porches to Heaven?

Where shall I part the branches of this hush
to spy you singing? Where
flies the song from the broken bird?

I call your name, but so softly
even my heart cannot hear me.
I should not like you to laugh,

even ever so gently.
Not but what you would pray, protect me,
do what you could—do all the blest dead's duties—

Nor would I pit No against Yes.
The truth is not found where platitudes clash,
but slips from their midst like Jesus.

Nor will I out of my mourning
maligning your merriment, twist
the fact of your pain into a jibe.

Yet after your unassuaged anguish of asking
I cannot, merely to solace my own,
make a cliché out of your death.

In Faith

FOR ANNE

Where none may come let roses go,
Urging the words lips cannot say.
Where heart may droop let roses blow
Over the sting and stun of day.
What heart must hide let roses show,
While faith must sleep let roses pray.

Where love sits still let roses fling
Aside the prim and proper rules.
When none dare breathe let roses sing
Defiance of all the sober schools.
While angels hang back, shivering,
Let roses rush, God's scarlet fools!

Elegy

FOR ROSA SELLS

No ghost crept in to tell me you were gone,
a ghost you would not credit anyway,
dispersing with a sniff black centuries
of Africa. (Or did—before you went
to your dark quiet, tidying up behind you
and troubling no one—did they howl around you,
sucking your breath, witch doctors hovered over
the frail sticks of your bones afire with fear,
the pale white faith fluttering from your fingers,
a handkerchief upon a hurricane?)
Only the light crept in instead of you.
I grieve, not for your death but for your life,
worked, like the flowers in your skimpy yard,
from lumpy clay. My race guilt I shrug off
as too abstract a tribute for a friend.
I view your untouched ironing with a sigh,
tug off the bed sheet you last week put on
and will no more, turning lady of leisure
lulled with this song of tired regrets as trite
as tears, as hackneyed as the human heart.

Addict

Each day I hacked out my heart
into black chips of words
until it was gone.

So, I snipped my heart from paper,
hurt in the hollow
where my real one was.

Now I sit idle, my hands
shaping wide arcs of nothing
serving as poems.

Entreaty

My thought clings to you
lest it slip away
into the darkness,

and there shiver, blind,
bone-cold, and in terror
like a lost child,

its blindness a dazzle
of the icy light,
the sterile glare

of stone, tree, and space
with me in the midst,
moth on a pin.

If, then, you should feel
a shadow's frail wing—
brush it off gently.

This Is the Way It Goes

The morning swoops to crush
Under its heavy heel
The shell of dream you wish
Had been spun out of steel.

Those ants inside the wall,
The minutes, pinch your brains
To animate your crawl
On stumps of aches and pains

Until the day has passed
Somehow, the dark piled deep
Around you when at last
You stumble into sleep.

Temporary Relief

My heart, a wintry forest,
had no sound but the leaves' crusty lips
till your foot among them made music.

My heart, a stony desert,
was barred with burning against all comers
till the spring wind of your breath sowed flowers.

My heart, a naked stranger,
crumpled broken along the roadside
till your fingers stopped its wounds bleeding.

I forbid my heart knowledge
that the silence, the drouth, and the hurt
assault me again with your going.

Ecclesiastes the Second

After a weary night of sleep,
Struggling across the jungle floor
Of dream—far better than to keep
Awake is to doze off some more.

After noon's heat subdues the birds,
Why match its fury in hot rages
Of verse and let a snarl of words
Mar the perfection of blank pages?

After an arduous day of toil
At doing nothing as an art,
A little liquor serves to oil
The creaking hinges of the heart.

After the evening sky expands
From dusk to darkness, waste no breath
Talking of love, the clock's slow hands
Will spin you fast enough toward death!

Renewal

The coming day,
the secret of a solitary bird,
becomes the common property of sparrows.

And I beneath
night's threadbare coverlet the dawn pulls back
wish his discovery had been kept hidden.

For as it is,
my heart remembers how it is the gage
measuring the gap of years between us.

Their number notched
upon my bones, my breath become once more
the wind that drags your name across my nerves.

And

And, you know, one time the roof came off
and I could see the inside
of everything and everybody,
including me

and God, and in was out and out
was in and up was down and down
was up and "Here kitty!" I told
lions and tigers

and, don't you know, they danced up and ate out
of my hand and no one else could see
they were just toms and tabbies and
I laughed and laughed

and poems sprouted out of my skin
that slap-happy time when I dreamed love growing
on trees as money doesn't and
my arm came off.

Modesty

Sweating a little, like a dewy apple,
As round and rosy, always a shade disheveled,
Of whom one thinks, "There goes somebody pleasant,
Not beautiful, of course, but with an air
Like a small tune half-forgotten."
                                    A little
Lovelier than beauty, your face revealed
Or hid the sun for me—though now no face
Does that—only the opening or closing
Of my own eyes—still if I were to see you
Passing alone the street, I would come stand
Before you, arms hung limply at my sides
To say, "I love you, but it doesn't matter."

The Farm

FOR NINA AND VAL

Where peace goes whispering by,
creaks in the turning windmill,
lows in the cattle;
where the hot light stretches over the fields
like a lazy cat;
where the clouds scatter
and graze like sheep on the barren skies,
but gather no rain;
where the darkness opens its fist
spilling stars and the wind;
where love has grown quiet,
assuming the shapes
of the soil and the rock and the tree—
here in this land
let me rest, rest, rest, oh, filling my heart
full of a sweet emptiness!

Sophistication

When I was a child
I thought that it rained
all over the whole wide world at once,
but now, having grown much wiser,

I know that my neighbor
can receive a deluge,
and my scrap of earth lie here gasping
like a fish tossed onto land,

or that when it pours,
it is no monsoon
with the trees before long dripping in sunlight
all in a sweat about nothing.

On Approaching My Birthday

My mother bore me in the heat of summer
when the grass blanched under sun's hammer stroke
and the birds sang off key, panting between notes,
and the pear trees once all winged with whiteness
sagged, breaking with fruit, and only the zinnias,
like harlots, bloomed out vulgar and audacious,
and when the cicadas played all day long
their hidden harpsichords accompanying
her grief, my mother bore me, as I say,
then died shortly thereafter, no doubt
of her disgust and left me her disease
when I grew up to wither into truth.

Slump

Suddenly everything stops
as the swift blood declines
to a sluggish ooze amid a swamp.

The mind and the senses drift
upon a casual wind
blowing, petals of a shattered rose.

The body, God knows why, creeps
along, some crazy creature
half an insect, half a tumbleweed.

Only the heart lies awake,
a naked nerve, an eyeball
staring from the socket of the darkness.

Philosophy of Time

The days creep on, and, if I pit my pain
against the minutes, only crawl the slower.
Yet I recall when I'd have crammed the hours
into some cul-de-sac where none could find them,
while they rushed past me toward their dreaded end.
It is my heart, dear heart, that clocks my coming
toward you as it clocked your going from me,
time moving in us, not we in time.
For time is like an angry little beast
clawing inside us, tearing us to shreds.
No man has seen him, no pendulum's
his picture, being but a clumsy symbol,
convenient construct, handy hypothesis
to be discarded on that very day
all such constructions are—when time collapses
like an accordion whose tune is over.

Unteachable

Heart has no history
being born every morning
after yesterday did not happen.

Who chronicles a dream?
Or on what dusty shelf
is a sigh or a smile stored away?

Pain sweeps down like the wind,
pleasure like rain, both tumbling
time on top of the illiterate heart.

Fait Accompli

I sit while loneliness
Seeps slowly through my skin.
Waiting, I try to guess
Which one of us will win—

I or the gaunt black wolf
Who crouches in some lair
Of corner, cranny, shelf,
Ready to pounce and tear.

What need to ask when vein
Has felt the burning claws
Slash open so that pain
Beats where the heart once was?

Toward the End

The heat still hangs heavy,
yet is frayed at the edges
by a cool breeze.

Cicadas fall silent
in the midst of their droning
longer and longer.

Their green a worn habit,
the trees' branches droop downward,
dreaming of winter

when all of their leaves
will lie scattered beneath them,
fruit for the wind.

And I sit and wonder
whether snow will have piled
peace on my heart.

Invocation

Unwinding the spool of the morning,
the cicada spins his green song,
dream deeper than sleep's,

drawing me back through the lost years,
fumbling an invisible knob
on a hidden door,

a door I have always known waited
if I could but touch it to substance
and out of enchantment.

Cicada, cicada, fey doorman,
loop my heart in your skein till
my foot finds your lintel.

THE WESLEYAN POETRY PROGRAM

Distinguished contemporary poetry in cloth and paperback editions

ALAN ANSEN: *Disorderly Houses* (1961)

JOHN ASHBERY: *The Tennis Court Oath* (1962)

ROBERT BAGG: *Madonna of the Cello* (1961)

MICHAEL BENEDIKT: *The Body* (1968)

ROBERT BLY: *Silence in the Snowy Fields* (1962)

TURNER CASSITY: *Watchboy, What of the Night?* (1966)

TRAM COMBS: *saint thomas. poems.* (1965)

DONALD DAVIE: *Events and Wisdoms* (1965); *New and Selected Poems* (1961)

JAMES DICKEY: *Buckdancer's Choice* (1965) [National Book Award in Poetry, 1966]; *Drowning With Others* (1962); *Helmets* (1964)

DAVID FERRY: *On the Way to the Island* (1960)

ROBERT FRANCIS: *The Orb Weaver* (1960)

JOHN HAINES: *Winter News* (1966)

EDWIN HONIG: *Spring Journal: Poems* (1968)

RICHARD HOWARD: *The Damages* (1967); *Quantities* (1962)

BARBARA HOWES: *Light and Dark* (1959)

DAVID IGNATOW: *Figures of the Human* (1964); *Rescue the Dead* (1968); *Say Pardon* (1961)

DONALD JUSTICE: *Night Light* (1967); *The Summer Anniversaries* (1960) [A Lamont Poetry Selection]

CHESTER KALLMAN: *Absent and Present* (1963)

PHILIP LEVINE: *Not This Pig* (1968)

LOU LIPSITZ: *Cold Water* (1967)

JOSEPHINE MILES: *Kinds of Affection* (1967)

VASSAR MILLER: *My Bones Being Wiser* (1963); *Onions and Roses* (1968); *Wage War on Silence* (1960)

W. R. MOSES: *Identities* (1965)

DONALD PETERSEN: *The Spectral Boy* (1964)

MARGE PIERCY: *Breaking Camp* (1968)

HYAM PLUTZIK: *Apples from Shinar* (1959)

VERN RUTSALA: *The Window* (1964)

HARVEY SHAPIRO: *Battle Report* (1966)

JON SILKIN: *Poems New and Selected* (1966)

LOUIS SIMPSON: *At the End of the Open Road* (1963) [Pulitzer Prize in Poetry, 1964]; *A Dream of Governors* (1959)

JAMES WRIGHT: *The Branch Will Not Break* (1963); *Saint Judas* (1959); *Shall We Gather at the River* (1968)